Prison Industrial Complex Explodes

PRISON INDUSTRIAL COMPLEX EXPLODES

A POEM

MERCEDES ENG

TALONBOOKS

Talonbooks
278 East First Avenue, Vancouver, British Columbia, Canada V5T 1A6
www.talonbooks.com

First printing: 2017

Typeset in Myriad
Printed and bound in Canada on 100% post-consumer recycled paper

Interior and cover design by Typesmith
Cover painting Solid Cement Indians (1998) by Lawrence Paul
Yuxweluptun. 213.3 × 164 cm, acrylic on canvas. Image courtesy the
Buschlen Mowatt Nichol Foundation and Macaulay & Co. Fine Art,
Vancouver, British Columbia

Talonbooks acknowledges the financial support of the Canada Council
for the Arts, the Government of Canada through the Canada Book Fund,
and the Province of British Columbia through the British Columbia Arts
Council and the Book Publishing Tax Credit.

Canada

Library and Archives Canada Cataloguing in Publication

Eng, Mercedes, 1972–, author
        Prison industrial complex explodes : poems / Mercedes Eng.

ISBN 978-1-77201-181-4 (softcover)

        I. Title.

PS8609.N43P75 2017   C811'.6   C2017-905263-2

for my nieces so that one day
they will know their grandfather

We operate in the teeth of a system for which racism and sexism are primary, established, and necessary props of profit.

—AUDRE LORDE
The Uses of Anger: Women Responding to Racism (1981)

Almost two million people are currently locked up in the immense network of U.S. prisons and jails. More than 70 percent of the imprisoned population are people of color. It is rarely acknowledged that the fastest growing group of prisoners are black women and that Native American prisoners are the largest group per capita.

—ANGELA Y. DAVIS
Masked Racism: Reflections on the Prison Industrial Complex (1998)

PRISON INDUSTRIAL COMPLEX EXPLODES

This year, July 21, 2013, will mark 25 years since the Canadian Multiculturalism Act received Royal Assent. This anniversary presents an opportunity to reflect on the past 25 years of reporting on the Operation of the Canadian Multiculturalism Act, and to look forward to the next 25 years of multiculturalism as an intrinsic part of Canadian society. As diversity challenges continue to change, multiculturalism in Canada has undergone several phases in its evolution over the course of the past four decades, including the celebration of differences through food and festivals, equity and tackling systemic discrimination, and working towards the full participation of culturally and religiously diverse communities in society.

This year, June 1, 2013, will mark the 40th anniversary of the Office of the Correctional Investigator. The Office of the Correctional Investigator was created in response to the *Report of the Commission of Inquiry into Certain Disturbances at Kingston Penitentiary*, which had identified the need for an independent body to review and provide redress to inmate grievances.

The Commission summarized the conditions at Kingston Penitentiary (KP) in April 1971 as "repressive and dehumanizing." Inmates rioted for four days. The KP riot was not isolated, but part of an escalating series of violent institutional disturbances in the late 1960s and early 1970s.

Though 40 years removed from the circumstances that gave rise to one of the most infamous prison riots in Canadian history, the Commission's assessment of what caused the riot remains remarkably relevant and prescient today:

> overcrowding, the shortage of professional staff, programming cuts, the confinement in the institution of a number of people who did not require maximum security confinement, too much time spent in cells, a lack of adequate channels to deal with complaints

SECTION 1

REFLECTION OF CANADA'S MULTICULTURAL REALITY
IN FEDERAL INSTITUTIONS

Q. 1.1

Does your institution's vision, mission, mandate, and/or priorities statement(s) include reference to multiculturalism?

Earlier this fall, the federal government hired auditor Deloitte to examine various international jurisdictions that have utilized the Public Private Partnership (P3) model for correctional facilities. PPP Canada is aiming to build its understanding of the various models, approaches, and experiences of P3 correctional facilities in a global context to determine their relevancy to the Canadian market. Of particular interest is the United States, which currently houses the largest prison population in the world and deploys inmates as a captive labour force.

Several private-sector operators of detention facilities are working to land contracts to operate Canada's immigrant detention centres, some of which are undergoing expansion. BD Hamilton and Associates lobbied the Conservatives to work with the Government of Canada to build a refugee detention centre in Toronto. Their proposal called for a P3 arrangement financed by the real estate developer.

Q. 1.2

Does your institution have policies
related to multiculturalism?

As companies move beyond the recession, the key challenges for business, HR, and talent are becoming clear to Deloitte. At the top of the list? Globalization, the drumbeat of technological change, intense regulatory environments, and the reality of distributed work in the cloud. The implications of these changes for human capital are profound.

Q. 1.3

Does your institution have programs related to multiculturalism?

As a full-service corrections management provider, Corrections Corporation of America specializes in the design, construction, expansion, and management of prisons, jails, and detention facilities, as well as inmate transportation services. We are the fifth-largest corrections system in the nation, behind only the federal government and three states. CCA houses nearly 80,000 inmates in more than 60 facilities, the majority of which are company-owned, with a total bed capacity of more than 90,000. CCA currently partners with all three federal corrections agencies (the Federal Bureau of Prisons, the United States Marshals Service, and U.S. Immigration and Customs Enforcement), many states, and local municipalities.

Since our inception, CCA has maintained its market leadership position in private corrections, managing more than 40% of all adult-secure beds under contract with such providers in the United States. The company joined the New York Stock Exchange in 1994.

We are proud of the distinctions of having been named among "America's Best Big Companies" by *Forbes* magazine and having been consistently named by *G.I. Jobs* magazine as a "Top Military-Friendly Employer."

Q. 1.4

Does your institution have reality-television programs related to multiculturalism?

The B.C. Civil Liberties Association says it plans to file a privacy complaint against the Canada Border Services Agency (CBSA) for allowing a reality TV show to film travellers crossing Canada's border without their free and informed consent.

The issue came to light after the CBSA allowed a TV film crew from the show *Border Security: Canada's Front Line* to film a raid on a construction site in Vancouver where immigration officials were looking for undocumented workers.

Q. 1.5

Did your institution undertake
initiatives to promote exchanges and cooperation
among diverse communities of Canada?

Carole is

Jessi's mama
now a ghost mama
whispering into the ears
of the fertile red nation

        plant seeds in the ground
        and in the womb
        ground zero for a revolution

she reads in the 2013 census report that since 2006
the Indigenous population increased from 3.8% to 4.3%
of the colonial nation
and she dances

knowing there are even more babies
ones who avoided becoming state stats
like Kanahus's freedom babies
unregistered babes taken to the woods
knowing this she dances
and she puts her back into it

JUNE 27, 1974

Mr. Donny LEE
Mountain Prison
Agassiz, B.C.

   Re: Your Deportation

Dear Donny,

At long last I have now heard from Ottawa regarding the
immigration department's position regarding the timing
of your deportation. Their position, as confirmed by the
head of the enforcement branch in Ottawa, is that they
will not seek to enforce the deportation order until you
have completed your sentence of imprisonment including
any period of mandatory supervision. What you will then
be able to do is that, after you have been out on the
street for some while and have established yourself, you
can then re-apply to the immigration appeal board for a
review of your case and try to persuade them to stay your
deportation again in light of your proven rehabilitation.

Yours sincerely,

Michael Jackson
University of British Columbia
Faculty of Law

my dad is inside when I am born. after I come out we live in Vancouver a bit then move to Abbotsford to be closer to the prison. we visit almost every weekend, both days, 8 hours a day. 832 hours in a year times 2. almost 70 days by the time I'm 2.

he gets out when I'm 2, but goes back because later I remember my mom saying I have a surprise for you and I think it's a record player. but it's my dad behind the door, home from jail. so he went somewhere between 2 and 7, somewhere with dinosaurs and a bumpy gravel road.

we are on the highway in Vancouver, starting our drive back home to Medicine Hat. the car stops suddenly and then there are two really angry men yelling, "open the fucking door!" they smash open the window and they're both grabbing my dad, one by the hair, the other by the throat. it looks like they wanna strangle him. my dad is kicking, he's fighting. but it doesn't work, they take him and he's gone.

there is a good time, we move to a bigger house. but something happens and my dad is gone again. but then he gets out and he is straightened out and he is working the gas fields and there is money and our allowance goes up and my little brother gets G.I. Joe everything for Christmas and my mom is happy.

we spend summer vacation at the women's shelter.

we run into an old friend visiting her new old man in Drumheller prison and when we go out for dinner after she makes me blush with her pronouncement that I'm "getting titties."

I'm 13 the next time my mom pulls the surprise-behind-the door trick and I feel sick.

at 15 and 16, I use my mother's visits to my father, the ones she makes me and my brother go on less and less frequently, as opportunities to run away from home, succeeding on the third try.

I'm 19 the last time I visit my dad inside, the last time he's inside, a prison 40 km away from the prison he escaped from just before he met my mother.

a tall tall fence
a jacket to throw over the barbwire
a haystack in a farmer's field overnight
a train ride a train track
a store selling used goods

a pregnant 19-year-old white girl and new charges

or

a strawberry-picking pass
a rumour about a prison labour stoppage
a train ride a train track
a store selling used goods

a pregnant 19-year-old white girl and new charges

SECTION 2

EMPLOYMENT OPPORTUNITIES IN FEDERAL INSTITUTIONS

Q. 2.1

Throughout your institution, does your workforce
represent Canada's diversity?

A strike by federal inmates over a cut in their pay that began in Ontario has now spread to prisons in New Brunswick, Quebec, and Saskatchewan. Inmates are protesting a 30% pay cut that took effect this week. The Harper government began deducting the money from prisoners' pay as part of a move to recover costs under the Deficit Reduction Action Plan.

Correctional Service Canada confirmed, "Work and program refusals are occurring sporadically across the country."

The average pay is $3 a day, a rate established in 1981 and based on a review by a parliamentary committee that also factored in a deduction for inmates' room, board, and clothing. Despite inflation over the past 30 years, inmates have not had a pay raise.

The strikes have also forced the shutdown of the government's CORCAN operations inside the prisons. CORCAN makes textiles, furniture, and other goods for the war machine.

A spokesperson for the Minister of Public Safety and Emergency Preparedness called the strike "offensive to hard-working, law-abiding Canadians."

Q. 2.2

How does your institution benefit from having
a multicultural workforce?

Federal Prison Industries (FPI) is a wholly owned, U.S. government corporation. Its mission is to employ and provide job-skills training to inmates confined within the Federal Bureau of Prisons; produce market-priced quality goods and services for sale to the Federal Government; operate in a self-sustaining manner; and minimize FPI's impact on private business and labor.

Inmates earn $0.23 to $1.15 per hour. They gain marketable job skills while working in factory operations such as metalwork, furniture, electronics, and textiles, producing goods for the military industrial complex.

A Business or Correctional Program?

FPI is, first and foremost, a correctional program. The impetus behind FPI is not about business, but about helping offenders acquire the skills necessary to transition from prison to law-abiding, contributing members of society. The production of items and provision of services are merely by-products of those efforts.

Who Are the Customers?

FPI is restricted to selling its products to the Federal Government. Its principal customer is the Department of Defense, from which FPI derives approximately 53% of its sales. Other key customers include the Departments of Homeland Security, Justice, Transportation, the Treasury, Veterans Affairs, and the Federal Bureau of Prisons.

Q. 2.3

How does your institution incentivize
a multicultural workforce?

The Mississippi Department of Archives and History states that Mississippi State Penitentiary, the oldest prison in the state and one originally designated for Black men, "was in many ways reminiscent of a gigantic antebellum plantation." The state was the first to implement conjugal visits, which were used as incentive to convince prisoners to work harder in their manual labour.

Well, eighteen hammers standing
Standing in a line
Well, there's eighteen hammers standing
Standing in a line

Well, they ring like silver, and
And they shine like gold
Well, they ring like silver, and
And they shine like gold

Well, one of them hammers you got
It don't ring like mine
Well, one of them hammers you got
It don't ring like mine

Well, I'll be living when
When you be dying
Well, I'll be living when
When you be dying

Well, I shot me a dead man, got
Got a hundred years
Well, I shot me a dead man, got
Got a hundred years

Well, I raise up my hammer, let it
Let it drop on down
Well, I raise up my hammer, let it
Let it drop on down

—Johnny Lee Moore and 12 Mississippi Convicts

**Royal Canadian Mounted Police /
Gendarmerie royale du Canada**
P.O. Box 1320
Edmonton, Alberta T5J 2N1

JULY 9, 1984

<u>WITHOUT PREJUDICE</u>

Mr. Sue Dong ENG
Medicine Hat, Alberta

Dear Mr. ENG:

This has reference to your complaint of December 8, 1983, regarding the possible theft of a gold necklace from your effects during escort.

Please be advised our investigation into your complaint is continuing and you may expect further correspondence in due course.

Yours truly,

Assistant Commissioner

Royal Canadian Mounted Police /
Gendarmerie royale du Canada
P.O. Box 1320
Edmonton, Alberta T5J 2N1

AUGUST 14, 1984

WITHOUT PREJUDICE

Mr. Sue Dong ENG
Medicine Hat, Alberta

Dear Mr. ENG:

This has reference to your complaint of December 8,
1983, alleging that our members were responsible for
the theft of your necklace. Following your complaint a
thorough investigation was conducted. I have now had the
opportunity to review the material.

The investigation revealed that your necklace did go
missing some time prior to, during, or after your escort
from Medicine Hat City Police Cell Block to the Lethbridge
Correctional Centre. However, the person(s) responsible
could not be determined. In my view there is no evidence
to support your allegation of theft.

Notwithstanding my decision in this matter, the criminal
allegation in your complaint was thoroughly reviewed by
a Senior Agent of the Attorney General's Department, who
agrees with my findings.

Your claim against the Force had been referred to the
Department of Justice for their review and decision.

Yours truly,

Assistant Commissioner

Department of Justice Canada
Royal Trust Tower, Edmonton Centre
Edmonton, Alberta T5J 2Z2

OCTOBER 11, 1984

WITHOUT PREJUDICE

Mr. Sue Dong ENG
Drumheller Correctional Institute

Dear Sir:

I refer you to an incident occurring on or about
December 8, 1983, wherein you have alleged the loss
of a necklace owned by yourself while you were being
transported from the Medicine Hat Police cells to
Lethbridge Correctional Centre. The Crown is prepared to
compensate you in the sum of $150.00 for the apparent
loss of your neckchain.

I have enclosed a form of Release in respect of the alleged
loss to be signed by yourself and a witness. Upon receipt of
completed Release, I will requisition and forward a cheque
payable to yourself in the sum of $150.00.

Yours truly,

Edmonton Regional Office

KNOW ALL MEN by these presents that Sue Dong Eng, of the City of Medicine Hat, in the Province of Alberta, does hereby remise, release, and forever discharge Her Majesty the Queen in Right of Canada, Her servants, employees, agents, and assigns, from all matters of action, claims, or demands, of whatever kind or nature that Sue Dong Eng ever had, has now, or can, shall, or may hereafter have reason by loss of property owned by Sue Dong Eng to wit: one gold or gold-coloured neckchain.

IT IS UNDERSTOOD AND AGREED that this Release shall only be effective when payment shall have been made on behalf of Her Majesty in Right of Canada to Sue Dong Eng the sum of One Hundred & Fifty Dollars.

the apparent loss
the alleged loss

a gold neckchain
a ligature
a tight rope
a border
a revocation

Her Majesty the Queen in Right of Canada wears a lovely
gold-plated neckchain of copper

SECTION 3

POLICIES, PROGRAM DELIVERY, AND PRACTICES

Q. 3.1

Did your institution develop
policies and programs that took into consideration
multiculturalism and diversity?

According to RCMP documents obtained through access-to-information requests, the federal government created a wide-ranging surveillance network in early 2007 to monitor protests by First Nations people, including those that would garner national attention or target "critical infrastructure" like highways, railways, and pipelines.

An RCMP slideshow presentation from 2009 shows the intelligence unit reported weekly to approximately 450 recipients in law enforcement, government, and unnamed "industry partners" in the energy and private sectors. The presentation states that the intelligence unit can "provide information on activist groups who are promoting Aboriginal issues within your area."

A series of "weekly situational awareness reports" from Aboriginal Affairs and Northern Development Canada reveals a rigorous cataloguing of Idle No More's activities. In addition to the Aboriginal Affairs reports, Canada's Integrated Terrorism Assessment Centre, which operates within the Canadian Security Intelligence Service (CSIS), prepared a threat assessment on Idle No More.

Q. 3.2

Does your institution
encourage employees to integrate
diversity and multiculturalism
into regular activities?

For Immediate Release: Unist'ot'en Camp Meets with RCMP

On September 1, 2015, Unist'ot'en and several Wet'suwet'en hereditary Chiefs met with the Superintendent Hilton Smee, critical incident commander of the Royal Canadian Mounted Police, who had requested the meeting to discuss the police presence on the Morice Road and issues surrounding the Unist'ot'en Camp. Since 2009, the Unist'ot'en have maintained a camp by Wedzin Kwah (Morice River) that is blocking seven pipelines that do not have Unist'ot'en consent to use their land. The Unist'ot'en have asked the Superintendent to provide the Unist'ot'en with notice prior to any planned police action to ensure the safety and security of those individuals present at the Camp, and in particular the children and elders. The RCMP are presently operating under the assumption that the Morice River Forest Service Road is a highway, which, under Bill C-51, categorizes the blockading of such roads as "national security threats." The Unist'ot'en explained why they do not agree with this categorization, based on several court decisions. No agreement was reached on this point. The Unist'ot'en continue to exercise their Aboriginal rights and title to their traditional territory, and are hopeful that the RCMP will work with them respectfully and maintain open lines of communication to ensure the safety of all.

Q. 3.3

Did your institution deliver
training to employees to
increase awareness and knowledge of
multiculturalism and diversity issues?

A high-profile $5.5 billion Enbridge pipeline that would carry tar-sands oil to the Pacific through northern British Columbia has hit a wall of First Nations opposition, whose constitutional and legal position a former Cabinet minister has called "very strong." In the same province, the Tsilhqot'in Nation have to date blocked the controversial New Prosperity gold and copper mine.

Q. 3.4

How many employees from your institution participated in multiculturalism diversity-training activities?

Prison Architect: the videogame that lets you build and manage a Maximum Security Prison!

As the sun casts its early morning rays on a beautiful patch of countryside, the clock starts ticking. You've got to crack on and build a holding cell to detain the prisoners that are trundling to your future prison on their yellow bus.

As your workmen lay the last brick, you don't have a moment to let them rest as they need to get started on the first proper cell block so you can make room for the next prisoner intake. Once they've all got a place to lay their weary heads, the fun can really start. You'll need a canteen, infirmary, and a guard room. Oh, and don't forget to plumb in a toilet, or things will get messy. But what about a workout area? Or solitary confinement cells?

Or an execution chamber?

In 2003, at the age of 14, Ashley Smith was confined to a youth detention facility for 1 month after throwing crabapples at a postal employee. The initial 1-month sentence lasted almost 4 years, almost entirely in isolation, until her death by self-strangulation in 2007. Though Smith was videotaped placing a ligature around her neck, guards did not enter her cell to intervene and 45 minutes passed before she was examined and pronounced dead.

From Mafia Dons to power-crazed senators, *Prison Architect* has them all!

To bring these characters to life, Introversion teamed up with an award-winning writer to produce an enthralling tale of corruption and human misery set against the background of the modern prison industrial complex.

Finished your Supermax?

Got guard dogs roving every corridor and prisoners eating out of your hand? Now you can live the horror by firing up escape mode and playing as a prisoner hell-bent on getting the hell out of Dodge. Dig a tunnel, go for the armoury, or start a riot and slip out in the chaos, it's entirely up to you!

a game a training device a service a business

Q. 3.5

How many employees from your institution participated in multiculturalism/ecological diversity-training activities?

we have berry patches here

we have medicine here

the bears live here

the moose live here

we live here

this is our food back here

—Freda Huson, Unist'ot'en clan spokesperson

Carole is

a ghost mama
whispering into the ears
of the fertile red nation

      plant seeds in the ground
      and in the womb
      ground zero for a revolution

Michael Jackson
University of British Columbia Faculty of Law
Vancouver, B.C.

January 23, 1985

Dear Sir,

We spoke last in 1974, at which time you represented me in deportation proceedings against me. In that year the B.C. immigration authorities were attempting to deport me. At that time, as a result of your representation the deportation order was defeated. I am contacting you now because the Calgary office of the Alberta immigration department sent representatives to see me to inform me that a hearing will be held in approximately two months' time to determine my status, my family's status, and whether I can be deported or not. When you represented me in 1974, I went by the name Don Lee, the name I assumed when my mother remarried. Since then I have taken the name I was born with, Sue Dong Eng.

To refresh your memory, I landed in Canada from mainland China. I entered this country under a Chinese Nationalist passport. Since leaving, China has become a communist country and I do not wish to return to such a country. I have settled in Canada, I have married a Canadian citizen, and we have two children. I am a property owner and a taxpayer, and have been for at least a decade.

I am now serving a 5-year prison term at Drumheller Institution. I look forward to hearing from you. I also look forward to remaining a Canadian citizen.

Sincerely,

Sue Dong Eng

a settler

a husband

a father

a property owner

a taxpayer

a no-good recidivist chink

2

PASSPORT
PASSEPORT **NO. GV 24779**

The Ministry of Foreign Affairs of the
Le Ministère des Affaires Etrangères de la

Republic of China requests all civil and military
République de Chine prie les autorités civiles et

authorities of Friendly States to let pass freely
militaires des Pays Amis de laisser passer librement

M _GAM HOE accompanied_
child SUE DONE ENG

nal of the Republic of China, going to
nalité chinoise, se rendant

NADA via U.S.A. and
necessary countries.

ord assistance and protection in case of
lui prêter aide et assistance en cas de
y.

This passport contains 28 pages
Ce passeport contient 28 pages

3

同行眷屬: 妻(原姓名)_____ 及子女 壹 人
Accompanied by his wife
(Maiden name)
Accompagné de sa femme_____
(née)
and by _____ ONE _____ child (children)
et de _____ ONE _____ enfant(s)

持照人簽名 (外文)
本証名者護照無效
Signature of bearer
Signature du titulaire } _____

February 14, 1985

Gloomy Future for Oil-Services Industry Seen: Analysts Forecast Shakeout, Cutbacks

Union Carbide to Resume Output of Poisonous Chemical Responsible for 2000 Deaths in India

Fish Treaty Ratification Sought: President Reagan Asks Senate to Ratify Salmon Treaty with Canada

Prisoner Work Plan Defended: California Governor Says, "I believe that every prisoner physically and mentally capable of working should be put to work and earn their keep just like the rest of us"

Dow Rises 21.31 to Set New Record as Stocks Surge in Final Hour

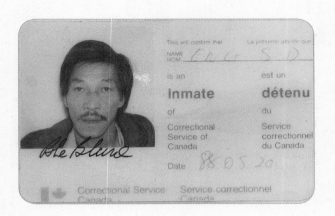

This will confirm that   La présente atteste que

NAME
NOM   ENG S D

is an   est un

Inmate   **détenu**

of   du

Correctional   Service
Service of   correctionnel
Canada   du Canada

Date   88 05 20

Correctional Service   Service correctionnel
Canada   Canada

THIS CARD WILL BE CARRIED AT ALL TIMES AND PRESENTED TO ANY
PEACE OFFICER ON REQUEST/LE LIBERE DOIT TOUJOURS AVOIR SA CARTE
SUR LUI ET LA PRESENTER SUR DEMANDE D'UN AGENT DE LA PAIX

Inmate No./No du détenu	Date of Birth/Date de naissance		
839303 —	17 JUNE 39		
Sex/Sexe	Weight/Poid	Height/Grandeur	Eyes/Yeux
M	120 lbs	5'6"	BROWN
Complexion/Teint		Hair/Cheveux	
Medium		BLACK	

SECTION 4

LANGUAGE AND CULTURAL UNDERSTANDING IN FEDERAL INSTITUTIONS

Q. 4.1

Has your institution undertaken
initiatives to incorporate the language skills of employees
from various backgrounds?

they let out Jessi's dad when Carole gave birth to
their daughter
beautiful Carole, paper-bag-coloured skin a black waterfall
of Pocahontas hair
Jessi was lucky to get a golden halo

Jessi's destatused mama died of the system
they let out Jessi's dad to look after her
once the price of her mama was extracted

I wonder how it is for beautiful
could-pass-for-a-white-girl Jessi
would-be-pheneticized-as-a-white-girl Jessi

Jessi who not only looked like a white girl
but the right kind of white girl
the kind of white girl boys and men go to war over
the kind of white girl who needs more lebensraum
the kind of white girl I used to wanna be

Q. 4.2

Did your institution undertake
initiatives to foster a corporate culture
that embraces diversity?

beautiful Carole

cocoa skin a black waterfall of Pocahontas hair

coffee skin black waterfall of Pocahontas hair

mahogany skin black waterfall of Pocahontas hair

cinnamon/nutmeg/clove skin
black waterfall of Pocahontas hair

brown sugar skin

copper skin

gold skin

they are washing beautiful Carole's
oil spill of Pocahottie hair
with cyanide
to get the gold from the ore

the poison begins to eat at her dreamcatcher bikini top
cleaving flesh from rib, her beaver-pelt bikini bottoms
stained with the fingerprints of corporate lunches
but she's gonna wash the man right out of her hair

this fantasy comes
with a Kleenex-feather headdress for easy cleanup
after, you can head directly to the drum circle
team-building exercise

Q. 4.3

Has your institution undertaken
initiatives to incorporate
the cultural insights of employees
to improve policy-making functions
and/or enhance service delivery?

she packs her lunch
beefalo sandwiches
spread with a semi-solid emulsion of
vegetable fats and chlorinated tap water
SPA493 apple slices with high-fructose corn syrup dip
man, this apple named after the language group of her people
tastes good

he goes out for dinner
Wind Cave bison carpaccio to start
squawb for the main
dessert is going to be sweet and dark
honeyed with a blood centre
stick-in-your-teeth meat

he bites down hard
on a shard of bone
crushing a molar
infection ensues

immune to the contagion
she is taking swimming lessons
breaststroking through slipstreams of capital's desire
hair garlanded with mutant *Corallina vancouveriensis*

SECTION 5

CONSULTATION AND COLLABORATION
WITH COMMUNITIES

Q. 5.1

Did your institution undertake
initiatives to improve federal services
for ethnocultural groups?

a partial commissary list for Metropolitan Detention Center, Los Angeles:

Timex watch	$36.40
Timex watchband	$11.70
watch battery	$2.60
prayer rug	$13.99
kufi (white)	$5.96
dhikr beads	$4.96
regular relaxer kit	$6.50
super relaxer kit	$6.50
Luster's Pink lotion	$4.95
Afro pick	$0.50
Afro comb	$0.55
hot waves brush	$2.75
dictionary	$1.95
envelope	$0.05
legal envelopes (3pk)	$0.80
writing pen	$1.20
writing tablet (legal)	$1.25
photo album	$3.45

Q. 5.2

Did your institution collaborate or partner
with ethnocultural community organizations
to help promote and deliver federal programs?

Surrey Pretrial Services Centre is presently undergoing a
$90-million expansion that includes 216 new high-security
cells with high-definition televisions and 100 new staff.

The B.C. Government and Employees' Union corrections
component chair said the jail currently has a ratio of
1 guard per 38 inmates, but the upgrade would change
that to 1 guard per 72 inmates.

"Our No. 1 priority is the safety of the officers. We'd like
to see resources go toward staffing, have proper staffing
levels, and have proper safety protocols."

He did however acknowledge that TVs in each high-
security cell play the role of unofficial "babysitter" to
inmates residing within.

Q. 5.3

Did your institution collaborate or partner
with ethnocultural community organizations
to help promote and deliver
federal reality-television programs?

The B.C. Coroners Service has confirmed that 42-year-old Lucia Vega Jimenez died in Canadian Border Services Agency (CBSA) custody. Jimenez was awaiting deportation to Mexico when she attempted suicide. She was found hanging from a shower stall in the immigration holding centre at the Vancouver airport, on December 20, 2013.

Jimenez had a job as a hotel worker in Vancouver when she was arrested over an unpaid transit ticket, transferred to jail, then sent to the CBSA holding cells at the Vancouver airport to await deportation.

Province of British Columbia — Ministry of Forests

UNIT CREW PROGRAM TRAINING ASSESSMENT

Crewman.

NAME	AGE	HEIGHT	WEIGHT	STATIONED
Eng, Don.	50	5'7	130	Elbow, LK.

TRAINING

☐ CATEGORY I TRAINING   ☑ CATEGORY III TRAINING   ☐ RECERTIFICATION

RATING

	UNSATISFACTORY	MARGINAL	COMPETENT	SUPERIOR	OUTSTANDING
1. ABILITY TO FOLLOW INSTRUCTIONS			✓		
2. RESPONSE TO DISCIPLINE		✓			
3. COORDINATION		✓			
4. CONFIDENCE		✓			

	UNSATISFACTORY	MARGINAL	COMPETENT	SUPERIOR	OUTSTANDING
5. SAFETY ATTITUDE		✓			
6. MATURITY		✓			
7. VIGOUR		✓			
8. ADAPTABILITY		✓			

PHYSICAL FITNESS TEST

INITIAL TEST: DATE June. 27. 1989   Level II   SECOND TEST: DATE _____

ACTIVITY	PASS	FAIL
SIT-UPS		
PUSH-UPS		
CHIN-UPS		
RUN TIME:		

ACTIVITY	PASS	FAIL
SIT-UPS		
PUSH-UPS		
CHIN-UPS		
RUN TIME:		

INSTRUCTOR'S COMMENTS:

INSTRUCTOR'S SIGNATURE	DATE Y M D	TRAINEE'S SIGNATURE	DATE Y M D
Neil Campbell	89 06 29	D. H. Eng	89 06 28

SUPERVISOR'S COMMENTS:

ACTION

☐ ISSUE CATEGORY I CREW LEADER CERTIFICATE
☐ ISSUE CATEGORY I CREW MEMBER CERTIFICATE
☐ ISSUE CATEGORY III CREW LEADER CERTIFICATE
☒ ISSUE CATEGORY III CREW MEMBER CERTIFICATE
☐ FAIL - TERMINATE
☐ FURTHER TRAINING
☐ OTHER

SUPERVISOR'S SIGNATURE	DATE Y M D
	89 01

FS 59 PRO 89/03

stationed

Kwìkwèxwelhp Healing Village is a minimum security institution for Aboriginal men built on traditional Chehalis First Nation land. Formerly called Elbow Lake Institution, it was renamed in 2001. *Kwìkwèxwelhp* means "where medicine is collected."

where labour is stationed

while Jessi is in belly, before Jessi's bug eyes can open
Carole shows her the world

Carole flies through a sky as big as an ocean
her oil slick hair streaming behind her for eight city blocks
murders of infant crows clutching strands of it

she sights the prison holding Jessi's daddy's body, mind,
and spirit
descends to his window

she hears him singing
"I Can't Get Next to You"
not like The Temptations, like Al Green
lower, lonely, filled with the longing that put Jessi in
Carole's belly

to his loves he sings

> I,
> oh,
> I,
> can turn a gray sky blue
> you see, I can make it rain when I want it to

to his call she responds

> I,
> I can fly like a bird in the sky

SECTION 6

DATA COLLECTION AND RESEARCH FOR POLICY AND PROGRAM DEVELOPMENT

Q. 6.1

Did your institution conduct research
with multicultural components?

Manitoba's Child and Family Services department seized
358 newborns, an average of one newborn every day,
between 2014 and 2015. The province has one of the
highest apprehension rates in Canada and it currently has
about 10,000 children in care, the majority of whom are
Indigenous.

In 2007, the First Nations Child and Family Caring Society
of Canada and the Assembly of First Nations filed a
human rights complaint alleging that Aboriginal Affairs
and Northern Development Canada provides deplorable
funding for child welfare on reserves, far below financial
support given to other Canadians.

In 2013, the Canadian Centre for Policy Alternatives
reported that 62% of First Nations children in Manitoba live
in poverty, are three times more likely to live in a house
requiring major repairs, and are five times more likely to
live in an overcrowded house compared to low income
non-Indigenous children.

60s Scoop
62% of red children
without adequate food water and shelter

means change genocidal intent constant

Q. 6.2

Did your institution undertake
other initiatives related to collecting statistical data?

This year's Annual Report from the Office of the Correctional Investigator calls special attention to the increasing diversity and complexity of prison demographics. In the 10-year period between March 2003 and March 2013, the incarcerated population has grown by close to 2,100 inmates, which represents an overall increase of 16.5%.

During this period, the Indigenous incarcerated population increased overall by 46.4%. Federally sentenced Indigenous women inmates have increased by more than 80% in the past 10 years. Visible minority groups behind bars have increased by almost 75%, while white inmates actually declined by 3%.

When combined, the number of Indigenous and visible minority inmates now exceeds 6,000 of a total incarcerated population of approximately 15,000. In other words, 40% of the inmate count on any given day now comes from a non-white background.

Disproportionate rates of incarceration of some minority groups, including Black and Indigenous peoples, reflect gaps in our social fabric and raise concerns about social inclusion, participation, and equality of opportunity.

first metal detector

first Halloween costume
  a white onesie with drawn-on black stripes
  father's prison ID no. 5915 on baby breast

first memory

first lesbians
  guards who were so kind
  let me bring in books to read
  though they weren't supposed to

first Waldorf salad

first exposure to art
  called Indian craft
  its production framed as money for the canteen

first exposure to my father's art
  also called craft converted to money for the canteen
  his cigarettes and my favourite, Big Chief beef jerky

        he carved the wooden tools
        he used to engrave
        owls mountain lions phoenixes wolves dragons
        into copper sheets hammered thin as his brown flesh

        homemade like the tools used to carve stories
        into thin brown flesh
        a tape-player motor a ballpoint pen

        homemade like the tools used to erase stories
        hammered into thin brown flesh and mind
        a light bulb filament to puncture the skin
        solace brought from outside inside a body

first horsey ride

first grim fairy tale
      two brothers came to the prison
      because they hurt a little girl
      she was too small for them so
      they made her bigger
      at lunch the guards walked out
      and the prisoners sent the brothers to the hospital

first shoes, made inside by my dad

I think about that yellow bead a lot

Carole researches
Group 4 Securicor (G4S)
the biggest private security group by revenue
the third-largest private employer
in the world

Carole learns
about G4S regulating prisons in Palestine
regulating security check points in American schools
regulating the U.S.–Mexico border

Carole laughs and cries
when she reads on the company's website:
In more ways than you might realize,
G4S is securing your world

Carole weaves
a G4S-resistant security blanket
big enough for all the babes of all the red nations

Carole swims
up Wedzin Kwah then lies on the roof
of the healing centre at the Unist'ot'en camp
to work on her spectral tan

Carole flies
north to the Lax U'u'la camp
at Lelu Island, the Flora Banks
where she lies with the salmon who rest
in the estuary's eelgrass beds
making ready for their transition from fresh to sea water
meditates on Bruce Lee and his one-inch punch
and being like water
then starts weaving a net to capture G4S execs
puts on headphones to speed her work
raps along with Nicki: first things first, I'll eat your brain

SECTION 7

SUCCESSES AND CHALLENGES

Q. 7.1

Does your institution face
barriers or challenges with respect to implementing
the Canadian Multiculturalism Act?

Terrace, British Columbia, was once the cedar pole capital of the world. More than 50,000 poles were manufactured annually to supply many parts of North America with telephone and electric power poles. Recently Terrace's economy has been forced to diversify since nearly all mills have closed down. The city envisions itself as a service hub for northwestern British Columbia, and looks forward to a bright future with Enbridge.

Q. 7.2

What initiatives does your institution plan to undertake
to further advance
the Canadian Multiculturalism Act?

John Paul, who suffered a brain injury while in Terrace RCMP holding cells, was just one Indigenous person injured in police-related incidents during a 3-week period. John George of Terrace received head injuries while a 15-year-old girl in Prince Rupert, British Columbia, suffered a broken arm.

Carole sings

Well, eighteen hammers standing
Standing in a line
Well, there's eighteen hammers standing
Standing in a line

Well, they ring like silver, and
And they shine like gold
Well, they ring like silver, and
And they shine like gold

Well, they'll be living when
When you be dying
Well, they'll be living when
When you be dying

Well, I raise up my hammer, let it
Let it drop on down
Well, I raise up my hammer, let it
Let it drop on down

SECTION 8

EVOLUTION OF MULTICULTURALISM
IN FEDERAL INSTITUTIONS

Q. 8.1

Considering
the Canadian Multiculturalism Act
and the evolution of multiculturalism in Canada,
how has your federal institution changed or evolved
to consider and respond to
Canada's increasing diversity
and to create an inclusive society in which
Canadians of all backgrounds
can participate?

Deloitte understands that in a rapidly changing global economy, companies face unprecedented challenges as the energy and resources industry undergoes dramatic change. Our Canadian oil and gas, utility, mining, and water companies are not immune to these challenges. Our industry business leaders recognize the difficulties of remaining competitive and thriving in today's market realities.

SECTION 9

REVOLUTION OF MULTICULTURALISM IN FEDERAL INSTITUTIONS

she's removed the greasy
manifestations of destiny
from her corporate Pocahottie bikini

stress has kept her jaw active
the years of pressure creating diamonds

when she goes to the city at night to eat
her incisors slice through the meat with ease

but hunting in the woods is better

she flies to Elsipogtog
setting her sights on the snipers
who situate their scopes on the Mi'kmaq warriors
the children, women, and men of the nation

she lowers herself into their crosshairs

she is a vision
wearing a feather headdress
that reaches the ground
her feet don't touch

each of the thousands of feathers
a spark to light the match

Carole sings

Well, I raise up my hammer, let it
Let it drop on down
Well, I raise up my hammer, let it
Let it drop on down

ACKNOWLEDGMENTS

Strangely enough, the government I critique so much
in this poem gave me a Canada Council for the Arts
grant to write it.

Thanks to the editors of *Line*, *The Capilano Review*,
The Volcano, *Tripwire*, and *Read Women*, where excerpts
of this poem first appeared. Thanks to *The Capilano Review*
for publishing a chunk of the poem in SMALL CAPS,
their multimedia chapbook series, to Madeline Terbasket
for singing on it, and to Damien Eagle Bear for
recording and mixing her beautiful blues voice.

Thank you to Eden Robinson, Harsha Walia, and
Tongo Eisen-Martin for blurbing this book. I admire
your work and ways of being in the world, and it
is such an honour to have you rep my work.

Thank you the people who provide the light when it is
dark: Annharte, Arlene Bowman, Candace Eng, Cecily
Nicholson, the Chinese seniors and youths fighting
for Chinatown where every member of the paternal
side of my family first lived when they arrived on this
shore, Cynthia Dewi Oka, David Jefferess, Downtown
Eastside warriors, Echo Kuo, Emily Fedoruk, Fred Moten,
Hari Alluri, Jake Kennedy, Jean Swanson, Jen Currin,
Karen Ward, Kathy Shimizu, Leslie Loubert, Lily Shinde,
Madeline Terbasket, the Women's Memorial March
Committee, Muriel Majorie, and my bebe, who builds the
city in the day then steals it back for me in the night.

NOTES ON SOURCES

Some parts of this poem weren't exactly written by me but consist of found and juxtaposed text. The numbered inquiries that structure the book are from a federal government questionnaire on the implementation of the Canadian Multiculturalism Act in federal institutions, including carceral institutions. I can't provide a link to this document because it was removed from the public sphere, like so many others, by the Harper government. The 2013 version of the questionnaire provides the poem's opening statement, and the text of the corresponding page is from the 2012–2013 *Annual Report of the Office of the Correctional Investigator*.

I answer each question with information on relevant subjects: government surveillance of Indigenous peoples' acts of land protection; PPP Canada, a federal Crown corporation that partners with private businesses to build public infrastructure like prisons and refugee-detention centres, private businesses that may have vested interests in the incarceration of Indigenous people fighting resource extraction; the mostly privatized U.S. prison system, which has the largest prison population on the planet, and where Black people and people of colour are disproportionately represented.

But even in answering these questions, the words are often not my own as I use text from the websites of corporations like Deloitte, Corrections Corporation of America (now CoreCivic), Federal Prison Industries, and even a video game company. Mostly I have left these texts intact. Also mostly intact are the many online news articles and news sources I read or listened to, and whose information I deployed in the service of exploding the system. In struggles for social justice, we must proceed as active learners. When reading the news I read widely, but take community-generated information as word. Check out the Facebook pages of the Unist'ot'en Camp and the Lax U'u'la Camp and YouTube videos for regular updates; the film documentary *Freedom Babies* about Kanahus Manuel, her babies, and her activism for the Secwepemc Nation; and any sources that have affected peoples speaking for themselves. This poem's reportage of land-defence camps is focused on

British Columbia, but there are many peoples defending the land in many places across the continent.

Other source texts, such as the commissary list for Metropolitan Detention Center, Los Angeles – California is the state with the highest number of prisoners – explicate the racial makeup of the prison population.

At times I use my father's words in his letters to prison justice advocate Michael Jackson. I have edited these slightly to protect the privacy of my fam.

Sometimes I use the state's images and words. The regulation of bodies across borders and the containment of bodies through prisons require identification. The state identification, Chinese and Canadian, is both intimate and reductive: the photographic portraits allow us to glimpse shimmers of my father's and grandmother's emotional states, while they are simultaneously reduced to date of birth, country of origin, physical information, passed medical exam. I found shocking the fact that the state had omitted mention that my dad was a prisoner when completing my dad's labour-capacity form. The Ministry of Forests's form uses the word "stationed" instead of "imprisoned" or "incarcerated," and even where he is "stationed" doesn't make clear his imprisonment: "Elbow Lake" is listed, not "Elbow Lake Institution." The letters from the RCMP and the Department of Justice in response to my father's claim that the RCMP stole his necklace also commit a gross omission. The correspondence does not admit the RCMP's crime, although my father is awarded money for his necklace.

Carole is inspired by an Indigenous mother I met while visiting my dad inside – one of a few destatused mothers I knew when I was a kid. But unlike the others, Carole did not live long enough to have her status returned to her when Bill C-31 amended section 12 of the Indian Act, which disenfranchised Indigenous women if they married non-status men. In reality she died of the system but in my dreams and in this poem she lives. Carole is also inspired by Annharte's *Cannibal Woman Camp Out*, a play about some of the many powerful and dangerous mythic mother figures from across this geopolitical entity called

North America who come together to attend a conference. The information that Carole provides on G4S is from Angela Y. Davis's *Freedom Is a Constant Struggle: Ferguson, Palestine, and the Foundations of a Movement.*

There are also song lyrics that Carole sings, from Al Green's "I Can't Get Next to You" to Nicki Minaj's killer verse in Kanye West's song "Monster," as well as Johnny Lee Moore with 12 Mississippi Penitentiary Convicts singing "Eighteen Hammers" as recorded on Alan Lomax's Southern Folk Heritage Series. "Eighteen Hammers" is a prison work song chanted to regulate the pace of work and to distract the workers from their labour. It is a call-and-response song, which by its nature is made individual and improvised by the singers even as some parts stay standard. So the lyrics included here are what I hear in recordings of the song. You may hear the lyrics differently.

The family photographs are mine. The whole time I visited my dad inside – from in utero to age nineteen – prisoners would go around taking photos of inmates with their families, and sometimes friends, charging a small fee like one or two dollars. These photos are so important because they provide inmates with a connection to the outside through their loved ones. Etheridge Knight's poem "The Idea of Ancestry" (1968) speaks to this experience, a fact not lost on Nicole R. Fleetwood, who references the poem at the opening of her beautiful essay on photography in U.S. prisons titled "Posing in Prison: Family Photographs, Emotional Labor, and Carceral Intimacy" (*Public Culture* 27.3 [2015]: 487–511). The prison photos included in *Prison Industrial Complex Explodes* are among my most beloved possessions now that my father is gone. I owe a huge debt of gratitude to these unknown photographers at all the institutions that ever imprisoned my dad. Thank you.

ABOUT THE AUTHOR

Mercedes Eng teaches and writes in Vancouver, unceded Musqueam, Squamish, and Tsleil-Waututh territories. She is the author of *Mercenary English* (CUE Books; Mercenary Press), a book of poetry about violence and resistance in Vancouver's Downtown Eastside. Her work has appeared in *West Coast Line*, *Canada and Beyond*, *The Capilano Review*, *Geist*, *Jacket2*, *The Downtown East*, and *The Volcano*. She is currently at work on a women's prison reader and a detective novel set in her grandfather's Chinatown supper club.